Journaling for People Who Hate Journaling

(Even Though They Know It's Good for Them)

Therapeutic Lists Workbook

Faith G. Harper, PhD, LPC-S, ACS, ACN
www.theintimacydr.com

Published by Say Something Real Press LLC.

ISBN-13: 978-0998889818
ISBN-10: 09988898914

So. Convince Me Journaling Is Good For Me.

Let me confess straight away. I fail at journaling. I have so many journals that I wrote a few pages in and then was completely over the process and stopped. If there were an NCAA tournament for journaling, I wouldn't make the 64. I wouldn't make the play-in. I wouldn't even make it to the NIT. Probably, I wouldn't even be allowed to buy a ticket to the game.

Unpacking my internal processes on paper? Not my thing.

Which is ironic because I KNOW how good it is for me therapeutically. Journaling prompts are something I assign my clients on the regular. Not because I am a cruel mistress, but because we are trying to figure out patterns in their thoughts and feelings and responses to what's going on in their lives.

Journal therapy is a legit thing. It's less about free-form writing and more about the *prompts*. In this particular version anyway. Free writing is also very therapeutic, so don't stop doing that if it works for you, boo!

Prompts just mean topics to write about. And these prompts are related to increasing your self-awareness, processing your thoughts, developing a stronger sense of self, tracking your progress, and promoting change.

Essentially, it's journaling with a point. And the point is to help you develop your emotional wellness.

Some of my clients take to journaling like they are naturals. Journaling makes sense for them, and they find the process healing. They feel better and I get the credit. I love it when I look like a brilliant therapist who knows what she's doing.

Some are more like me, and it is painful and uncomfortable and more like *seriously-can-we-just-do-shock-therapy-instead*? Here, I'll stick my finger in this light socket myself…just please don't ask me to journal.

Journaling can be overwhelming. Especially if you hate writing. Or, more to the point that you hate writing about yourself.

(Because I am writing right now, and it's all good. But if I had to write my fears for the future or something similar I would immediately go into *hot-water-burn-baby* panic mode. It's all so....messy. And raw. And gross.)

Then I figured something out that worked for me. And it worked for my journal-defiant clients.

Lists.

Lists are easy. We're all list makers to some extent. Tasks that must get done. Things that need to be purchased at the grocery story. This is probably why list journals have become popular in recent years. And a lot of them are pretty cool. But they are more focused on idea generation, creativity, etc. Planning meals and trips and classes.

Not so much list making for a therapeutic effect.

So that's what this workbook is about. Combining the concept of list journals with the concept of therapeutic journaling to create something that *even people-who-hate-to-write-so-much-please-don't-make-me* can utilize and benefit from.

But whyyyyyyy didn't you make this a digital workbook. Or an app. Bluetooth enabled so I could to speech-to-text list making while driving to work.

Sorry. I didn't. Because guess what is even better than journaling?

Journaling by hand.

Writing by hand is pretty unique in an era where we carry around tiny computers in our pockets at all times (that apparently can also be used to make phone calls, I hear?).

Writing by hand does different things to the brain.

It activates more of it. You remember more of what you write (sorry, laptop note takers).

AND it reduces anxiety and depression (because you are engaging areas of the brain known as the "writing circuit."

Activating the writing circuit *literally* (and I am literally using literally correctly here!) simmers down the part of your brain that is reinforcing depression and anxiety because you are increasing your focus on the task at hand.

So you have enough prompts here to do a list a week, plus more. It doesn't start with gut-wrenching stuff. It actually starts more like a regular list journal. Except you are going to use those lists to look for patterns of things that have meaning for you. And then some digging deeper stuff. But with the goal of making connections to the here-and-now and feeling better, stronger, and more present.

No weeping on Freud's sofa for years on end, I promise.

And for those of you that are interested? There are tons of references on the efficacy of journal therapy at the end of this workbook. This is legit science, not woo-woo.

And this particular workbook is designed to work with a number of evidence based treatment approaches, including: Cognitive Behavioral Therapy, Dialectical Behavioral Therapy, Acceptance and Commitment Therapy, and Solution Focused Brief Therapy. It also is a great compliment to somatic and relational based therapeutic practices in a multitude of ways.

Now, get to work!

My Favorite Movies

...any themes here?

My Favorite TV Shows

...any themes here?

My Favorite Music

…any themes here?

My Favorite Books and Other Reading Materials

...any themes here?

My Favorite Art and Artists

Stuff I Notice In Common Across These Lists of Creative Arts

Things I Have Learned (About the World, About Others, About Myself) From These Creative Arts

Ways I Have Grown as A Result of Having These Art Forms In My Life

Characters I Connect With in Books, Movies, and TV Shows

What I Like About These Characters

How I Am Like These Characters Already

The Things I Admire That I Would Most Like To Bring Out In Myself

Real-Life People I Admire Most
(Either That I Have Met Or Haven't Met)

What I Like About Them

The Ways in Which I Am Already Like Them

The Things About Them I Would Like To Bring Out In Myself

I Need

I Want

What Nourishes Me/Gives Me Energy/Keeps Me Going

Who Nourishes Me/Gives Me Energy/Keeps Me Going

The Things That Are Most Important to Me

The People That Are Most Important to Me

The People Who Support Me the Most

Places That Soothe Me/Restore Me/Help Me Feel Safe In The World

- MY BED
- THE BATHTUB
- THE BEACH
- THE ROAD

Places I'm Pretty Sure I Would Love to Visit

Things I Would Do on My Ideal Day

Ways These People And These Activities Make Life Worth Living For Me

My Core Values

The Situations That Make It Easiest For Me To Live By These Values

The Situations That Make It More Difficult

The Skills I Want To Cultivate To Better Live My Values

The Things Provide Me a Sense of Safety and Security

...Am I getting enough of these things in my life?

Things That Are in My Control

Things That Are Out of My Control

People I Want To Forgive And What I Want To Forgive Them For

People I Wish Would Forgive Me And What I Wish They Would Forgive Me For

Things I Want to Forgive Myself For

What I Miss About the Past

What I Appreciate in The Present

What I Most Hope for In the Future

Things I Can Do for Others TO Make Their Lives Better

Things I Can Do for Myself To Make My Life Better

Losses and Pain from Which I Have Healed
(...at least mostly)

Losses I Am Still Grieving And Pain I Am Still Experiencing

What I Need to Help My Grieving

Fears I Have Overcome

Things I Refuse To Feel Guilty For

How Do I Notice That I Am Stressed?

In My Body	In My Behaviors	In My Thinking

Things I Am Holding On To That I Need (or Want) To Let Go Of

Things I Need To Pay More Attention To

Things I Need to Pay Less Attention To

The Gifts I Have To Share With The World
(The Things I Was Put On The Planet To Do)

What I Need to Maximize These Gifts

The Achievements/Accomplishments That (Help) Define Me

The Achievements I Want To Tackle Next

What I Need To Make That Happen

Negative Messages I Received From Others In The Past

Negative Messages I Catch Myself Saying To Myself

...any overlap?

Healthy Ways I Can Take Care of Myself

...likelihood of me using these skills when I am stressed out?

Things I Can Do That Will Make It More Likely Take Care of Myself In Healthy Ways

Types of Movement I Enjoy
(How I Play)

Things That Are Getting in The Way of Me Playing

Things I am Doing Instead of Playing

Ways I Can Increase My Play Time by at least 10%

Things in My Life That Are Working Well
(Things That Don't Need to Be Changed or Fixed)

...Percentage of My Life Filled with These Working-Well Things?

Situations I Have Come Through That I Didn't Think I'd Survive

The Skills I Used To Get Through Them

The Skills I Have That Might Be Usable In Getting Through My Current Challenges

What Skills Do I Want to Learn To Help Manage Future Challenges?

References

Adams, K. (1999). *A Brief History of Journal Therapy.* Retrieved from http://journaltherapy.com/journal-to-the-self/journal-writing-history

Adams, K. (2003). *The Way of the Journal: A Journal Therapy Workbook for Healing.* Baltimore, Maryland: The Sidran Press.

Adams, K. (n.d.). *Journal Writing: A Short Course.* Retrieved January 03, 2018, from http://journaltherapy.com/journal-cafe-3/journal-course

Baikie, K. A. & Wilhelm, K. (2005). *Emotional and physical health benefits of expressive writing.* Advances in Psychiatric Treatment, 11(5), 338-346. doi:10.1192/apt.11.5.338

Camilleri, V. A. (2007). *Healing the Inner City Child.* London, England: Jessica Kingsley Publishers.

Dean, J., Potts, H., W. W., & Barker, C (2016). "Direction to an Internet Support Group Compared With Online Expressive Writing for People With Depression And Anxiety: A Randomized Trial". JMIR Mental Health 3(2). doi:10.2196/mental.5133.

Epple, D. (2007). "Journal Writing for Life Development." *Advances in Social Work. 8*(2) (2007): 288-304.

GoodTherapy.org. (n.d.). *Journal Therapy.* Retrieved January 03, 2018, from https://www.goodtherapy.org/learn-about-therapy/types/journal-therapy

Krpan, Katherine, et. al. (2013). "An everyday activity as a treatment for depression: The benefits of expressive writing for people diagnosed with major depressive disorder". *Journal of Affective Disorders. 150.* doi:https://dx.doi.org/10.1016/j.jad.2013.05.065

Murray, B. (2002). Writing to heal. *Monitor on Psychology, 33*(6). Retrieved from http://www.apa.org/monitor/jun02/writing.aspx

Oppenheimer, D. M., & Mueller, P. A. (2014). The Pen is Mightier than the Keyboard: Longhand and Laptop Note-Taking. PsycEXTRA Dataset. doi:10.1037/e502412013-155

Pennebaker, J. W. (1997). "Writing about Emotional Experiences as a Therapeutic Process." *Psychological Science. 8* (3): 162–166. doi:10.1111/j.1467-9280.1997.tb00403.x.

Pennebaker, J. W. (2010). "Expressive writing in a clinical setting". *The Independent Practitioner. 30*: 23–25.

Pennebaker J. W., Beall S. K. (1986). "Confronting a traumatic event: toward an understanding of inhibition and disease". Journal of Abnormal Psychology 95 (3): 274–81. doi:10.1037/0021-843x.95.3.274.

Pennebaker J. W., Kiecolt-Glaser J. K. ,& Glaser R. (1988). "Disclosure of traumas and immune function: health implications for psychotherapy". *Journal of Consulting and Clinical Psychology. 56* (2): 239–45. doi:10.1037/0022-006x.56.2.239. PMID 3372832.

Pennebaker, J. W., & Smyth, J. M. (2016). Opening up by writing it down: how expressive writing improves health and eases emotional pain. New York, NY: The Guilford Press.

Silver, J. (2016, October 18). 9 Incredible Ways Writing By Hand Benefits Our Bodies And Brains. Retrieved December 19, 2017, from https://www.littlethings.com/benefits-of-writing-by-hand/

Thompson, K. (2010). *Therapeutic Journal Writing: An Introduction for Professionals.* London, England: Jessica Kingsley Publishers.

Woolston, C. (2000). *Writing for therapy helps erase effects of trauma*. Retrieved January 03, 2018, from http://edition.cnn.com/2000/HEALTH/03/16/health.writing.wmd

90031572R00043

Made in the USA
Columbia, SC
24 February 2018